Living
The
American
Dream

By

Tim Dannelly

ISBN: 1-4140-1988-2 (e-book)
ISBN: 1-4140-1987-4 (Paperback)

Library of Congress Control Number: 2003097984

This book is printed on acid free paper.

Printed in the United States of America
Bloomington, IN

1stBooks - rev. 10/27/03

Dedicated to those great Americans who start at the bottom and work their way to greatness

Thank You

To Frances Wilkins for carefully proofreading each page and enduring all the rewrites.

To Brian Dannelly and Mike Dannelly for giving me first-hand experience with effective personal leadership techniques and for growing into men that make their dad proud.

Chapters

Preface

In New York Harbor is a place called Ellis Island. It's merely a museum today with larger than life pictures of the huddled masses yearning to breathe free, but some of your ancestors probably came to our shores through that portal. It's strange, isn't it, that Ellis Island's warehouse for human processing stands in the shadow of the beautiful Statue of Liberty. The dream of liberty and freedom that fills the hearts of immigrants sailing past the lady in the harbor becomes a shocking reality as one enters the Ellis Island buildings. In just minutes, a dreamy pilgrim moves from the deck of a ship to the line where they are classified and processed. Then the work begins. If one is to eat, one must work (even in America).

Immigrants faced the same reality in America that they faced in their homeland. America had poverty, bad weather, customers who didn't buy, employers who didn't hire and taxes. But the immigrants came here by the endless boatloads because America had limitless opportunity. It still does. And they still come. The dream of accomplishing great things is realized every day here in the land of the free.

For years, people in search of a better life have left their homeland and their kin in search of the American Dream. Every day, those of us born here in The United States of America take for granted all the opportunity and freedom made available to us. We think nothing of crossing a state line on a shopping trip. Without government approval, we openly attend a revival meeting at a neighborhood church. Without fear, we watch military planes leave their vapor trails across the skies and go routinely about our daily activities. We bravely travel hundreds of miles on the Interstate highways to visit clients as we compete for their business. Fewer than half of us routinely vote on issues and candidates. If those in public office disappoint us, we write letters to our newspapers or call a talk show and speak our piece! Once or twice in our lives, we may even express disagreement with government policies in an open televised meeting.

Nowhere is the American Dream more real than in the marketplace. Someone in your family has probably started at the bottom and worked his or her way to the absolute top. Perhaps you started as a wage-earning employee and have now moved into management. This is a routine occurrence here in America! It happens every day! We in America are limited only by our thinking and willingness to act.

Many great Americans had no idea or intent of moving into management at some point. We got a job because we wanted money and all the things it could buy. In the process, though, we discovered a love for what it was we did for that money. And we excelled. And company leadership gave us a raise and asked us to move up into a leadership role.

Some of us failed to succeed in the leadership of an organization where we once were the bright shining star. Perhaps this is one of those times when we have thought of it as the great American Nightmare! If we had only stayed out of management! Some people reading these words have experienced this agony on more than one occasion. Or perhaps you're in the pits of it right now! Even worse, perhaps you're managing the efforts of several people successfully and you have no idea why everything is moving along smoothly. If anything different comes your way, you remain calm on the surface but you worry about your future as the leader. Each time you see a young star emerge from college, you cringe in fear. After all, young people are so smart and educated! And you are just a hard working person who survived all the cuts and changes.

Many leaders with degrees in Business Management feel the same concerns! You are a leader today because, in the opinion of leadership, you were the best qualified at the time of the opening. You continue to lead because people (including leadership) don't like to fix things that aren't broken!

There are no magic formulas in these pages. The author is no genius who has made millions or become famous. He is merely a man who believes in the true American Dream, appreciates the price that has been paid to preserve it and the right of every citizen to seize it.

Far too many people only reach for a small part of what our free enterprise system offers to everyone who lives here. This book is dedicated to the great Americans who see the opportunity and are prepared to go for it all! If you are higher up the ladder of responsibility in your company than when you started or if you have a wish to step up, this is your book.

Success is not only for the

rich and famous

Chapter one

What Is Success - Really

You certainly don't remember the day you were born. That's impossible! But you may have heard about the circumstances of it all. As a tot and small toddler, things happened to you that the family still talks about. Your memory may go back to the first day of school in the first grade. You may recall the teacher vividly. You may remember the friendships you cultivated in the early elementary school years. Some of these may be with you to this day.

Junior high and high school seem to be a threshold for fond memories. Whether you're eighteen or eighty, you have some fond memories of those. Perhaps it's your first kiss or your first date. Could it be the championship game or the award you earned? For some of us, it's the night we were touched by the 'long arm of the law' or, worse, some tragedy that brought home to us the mortality of this life.

Early adult years bring memories home by the truckload. Good memories, like the freedom and excitement of college or a military enlistment, fill your memory bank with stories that your friends and family know by heart, they've heard them so often. Your first real job affords you the opportunity to have a nice car, nice apartment and the resources to save and even invest. You meet your Soulmate and find a love that is deeper than you imagined could ever exist. On the other hand, difficulty and heartache seem to be deeper in the adult years than any child could imagine. Your heart is broken, you are humiliated and you learn a new application for the word *hopeless*. You make a mistake at work and it results in your being passed over for a promotion or, even worse, you are fired. Financial challenges come your way. An unexpected expense throws you for a loop. You would have been wiped out, except for some quick thinking on your part and the fact that your credit limit was high enough to cover things. A potential embarrassment is averted by the fact that you were transferred in the nick of time.

As you have shared your life experiences with people, has anyone ever told you that your life story had the potential of being a best selling movie? Then take heart, friend, you are human! The greatest story will never be fully told—it is YOUR story! You were there when the great accomplishment came and there was no one to tell. You were there when the roof came crashing down on your head and you were able to pull things together so that things appeared normal again. You got no help because your pride, or lack of ability to express yourself, kept you from telling anybody what you were going through. You were the one who had to pick yourself up, dust yourself off and go on with life. As a matter of fact, you continue to be amazed, proud and ashamed when you look at your best selling movie.

You have had many successes in your life. Your maturity, your position with your employer or the growth of your own business, the progress of your family, your resolution to include God's will in your decisions are all signs of your own success. If you and I sat down together for a frank talk about your success, you couldn't tell me how it was that you became successful. You could tell me about events in your life or positive opinions that others formed about you but you would be hard pressed to put your finger on the exact thing that brought you such a wonderful life as you have today. Successful people are too busy living it, being it and doing it to notice and make a note of the exact steps involved in their success. That's greatly because many successful people don't consider themselves to be successful.

What defines "success" for you? Is it money or the things that money can buy? I think not! If that were the case, poor people would be miserable and wealthy people would be happy. There would never be a person with a low-paying job, serving as a non-paid Sunday school teacher and influencing the lives of many. Wealthy people would never enter into lawsuits or get divorces. Money isn't the answer. Wise old King Solomon wrote in one of his books *"he who seeks silver will never be satisfied with silver"*. No matter how much money you've earned, won or inherited in your life, you probably want more. Why else would you place it in an interest-bearing account or invest it in growth funds?

Is real success *fame*? No! Your own story is an amazing recount of how you overcame overwhelming odds to do great things. The precious moments you have spent with your Soulmate are more romantic than the most intense love story ever to be filmed. They exceed all words! Yet, you'll not likely see any of this on television or in the movies. Our society has become one that recognizes the bizarre. Rob a bank or kill several people and everyone wants to know if you're writing a book during your two years in prison. Raise your family, attend church, be a good neighbor, pay your taxes and you are far too boring to waste a line of print or a moment of airtime on. Fame doesn't often accompany real success.

Earl Nightingale, noted author and speaker, says real success is best described as setting a goal and going for it. If that's the case, are you a real success? Why do you go to work each day? Why are you trying so diligently to do well in your chosen profession? Why is it so important for you to buy a certain car or live in a particular neighborhood? When you finally get what it is you're working so hard to get, how do you finally feel?

Why do you go out of your way to be nice to those people you're trying to fit in with? Suppose you become one of them. Is that enough, or is there yet another plateau of Lords and Ladies to whom you must suck up? And if they don't give you the nod for your efforts, is it "off with your head"?

Look again at the theory "Success is setting your goal and going for it". That theory may just be right. Goal-oriented people never let things get them down, they just keep moving toward the goal. People who are goal-oriented never consider themselves as failures, even if the goal they pursue requires years of trying again. People who are in pursuit of their own goal aren't concerned with the size and fairness of acquisition of the goals of other people.

Perhaps another way of defining success is in HOW you pursue your life's goals. Successful people seem to be easy to spot because they have certain tendencies. They have, for instance, the uncanny knack of being able to make other people feel their own zeal for projects and ideas. Not all successful people are in Sales careers, but all successful people DO sell! You'll not likely find a truly successful person steamrolling their way over their peers and subordinates. Maybe you've been told that real successes push their weight around and force people to comply or lose. That simply isn't true. Though the bullies of industry CAN get away with forcing people to accommodate them a time or two, sooner or later people usually find a way to beat the boss's system. Truly successful people are followed and respected because they are busy, instead, convincing their followers to get on board. Successful leaders know every benefit the followers will gain by following, and those leaders can't wait for the followers to win! In this pattern of pulling for the worker to win, the successful leader even gains valuable input from workers who usually only react to orders. The bullies of the workplace refer to these successful people as people pleasers. By the way, those same bullies usually end up *working for* the pleasing successful people.

Successful people aren't geniuses, but they do posses a great deal of common sense. They realize people remember events and statements that stand out from the day-to-day events of life, so they conduct great meetings, using all sorts of visual aids and sound effects. It's difficult to forget an awards ceremony presided over by one of these great leaders. Successful people NEVER have stupid people working for them. As a matter of fact, they frequently tell their followers just how smart they are, and for the most unnoticeable things! Think of it, the leader praising the follower!

Tell a successful person he or she is different or even weird and they might even smile! He or she prides themselves on the fact that they march to a different drummer. Of course, all their individuality usually results in great accomplishments.

Did you ever meet a person who was convinced he was 'great', and took great joy in telling everyone just how remarkable he was? Amazingly, a successful person very seldom "blows his own horn". While he spends a great deal of his time praising and building up the people around him, he talks very little about himself. He always does his best and puts his best foot forward, but he actually seems uncomfortable when praises come his way!

What do you think of when someone refers to a person as a "company" person? Do you visualize that person following the boss around, always agreeing with any idea that is sent down from 'headquarters', working hours upon end for free? Believe it or not, our society has come to the place where that picture best defines company people. Some people actually do work with a set of ethics like that, and become frustrated beyond words. No company or leader is perfect. We are all human!

If you're smart, you'll get an education! If you're smart, you'll learn how to do your boss's job. Sooner or later, one is required to work. Do you know all there is to know about your job? Are you in the process of learning all there is to learn? And how much knowledge is necessary to assure you'll have a job in another five or ten years?

As you've been reading, you've no doubt pictured some successful person in your organization, or yourself, as you've let all this information into your mind. You may even think, "This is too simple so far. There has to be some secret formula to help someone achieve true success". While it may be true that certain achievements in this life require magic formulas, happiness and personal success are available to you right now on the simplest of terms! This minute! Who knows? You may already have them!

Nothing happens until somebody sells something

Chapter two

Getting Your Ideas Sold

If you tend to gravitate toward positive people, if the slouchy negative type gets you down, you probably have a lot of friends and associates in the sales business. *Successful* salespeople are a lot of fun. They're always "up" and they always seem to have the latest, hottest "deal' for you. They have this overwhelming "in charge" persona that makes you want to follow them wherever they're headed, or simply 'hang around' with them. *Successful* salespeople never seem to worry about "what if'. They always seem pleased because things constantly turn out their way! You can't possibly stump a successful salesperson.

Visit any part of the open marketplace of America and you'll find these movers and shakers at work in their element. They seem to love to seek out problems so they can solve them. Tell them their product or service won't do the job and they'll customize it for you so that it does. Tell them you can't afford it and they'll show you so many financial options, you may even buy two! They openly admit the competition's product or service is of the very best quality, almost as good as theirs! Try to insult them and it doesn't deter their driven attitude. You can't run them off with insults, cheaper prices from competitors or even your own reluctance to make a decision. They continue to pull for you to win until you DO win by purchasing their product or service.

Is it any wonder that those in the fields of Marketing and Sales generate the bulk of America's cash flow! They know exactly where they're going, they listen carefully to your expectations and make sure you understand the overwhelming reasons you should decide to make this purchase now not later and, best of all, *successful* sales professionals make it easy to do business with them. Time after time, you actually end up with a better product than you had expected when you do business with one of these successful professionals.

Successful selling requires patience and a selfless attitude. Successful salespeople must remain focused on the customer's best interest and must realize the customer isn't going to write the check until they clearly see the product or service filling their wants and needs. Americans have become very skeptical and demanding shoppers. The successful salesperson realizes this and patiently answers countless questions. You may have been in a transaction with one of these professionals and noticed how they make you feel as though you are their only customer! Of course you know they're very busy, but they're never too busy to give you the attention your transaction deserves.

Many salespeople are less than successful, though. Take the high-pressure sales person. We all get tired of pushy salespeople. Who wouldn't! They're pushy because they don't know enough about you, or about their product or service, to tell you what's in it for you and to let you make your own decision. They're too busy trying to trick you into a quick decision in THEIR favor, not yours! They push the product with the highest bonus that day. You begin to feel like you're being run through a burger drive-through when you encounter one of these sharks ("just tell me what it's gonna take, then get moving...I have other people waiting")! And they have a thousand different ways to talk you into a quick decision. Whatever you do, don't try to go home and think about it unless you want them to hound you for days.

How is it that we Americans love to buy things (and we buy so MANY things) when it's not always that much fun to purchase? Simple! We either find a salesperson we're comfortable with and stick with him, or we work out some other system and endure the process in order to get the product or service we want. Americans have a reputation for getting what we want!

The field of sales has been complicated by the less-than-professional-people working in it. The field of leadership and management has been equally corrupted.

Many organizations have promoted outstanding followers to positions of leadership, without the benefit of proper training. This is like taking the best member of a construction crew and making him a salesman for the homebuilder he's been working for. He's a proven company man, committed to getting the job done, even when conditions are uncomfortable! He respects the authority of those who tell him to "sell and produce a profit". Yet, if the construction worker isn't blessed with the personality of a salesman, he's destined for failure until he becomes trained in the art of selling. Managers require training and experience, just like skilled workers do.

Great Leaders Are Great Motivators

Leaders are a great deal like salespeople. The salesperson marries a product with a customer. The leader marries a task with an employee. Salespeople motivate buyers by showing them how they will benefit by purchasing a product. Leaders inspire followers by showing them how they will benefit by accomplishing a task or by reaching company objectives.

The term 'marry' involves a lot more than simply "hooking up" two people. Those two people need to know a great deal about each other. The more they know about each other, the more successful the marriage is destined to be. So it is in the world of leadership. The more leaders know about followers, the easier it is to lead them. This is true, even if the information about the followers is depressing or intimidating. One of the most frequent quotes by leaders who are being fired is, "I had no idea". "I had no idea that was going on" or "I had no idea the people were doing that" or "I had no idea they felt that way". Shock is a typical response from a relieved leader.

While leaders are professional communicators, followers are not. Getting to know your followers involves more than a simple conversation where the follower tells you his philosophy about life and what it takes to get him excited about performing a particular task. Many followers simply don't know what it takes to get them motivated. Though listening to your people is important, it isn't enough.

Do you remember your first job? When you had an opportunity to talk with your boss, how candid and honest were you? The intimidation of management types in the workplace inhibits honesty, sort of like the presence of a salesperson on a car lot. There's just a certain part of us that won't tell the whole story to a salesperson because we don't trust them with the information. Likewise, followers tend to talk differently to management. Great leaders cultivate the ability to listen between the lines. What's the follower's intent? How does he seem to feel about certain subjects? Have you ever commented, "It's not what he said, it's what he *didn't* say"? You were listening between the lines. You were listening to the intent of the person doing the talking.

Great leaders are responsible for the productivity of followers while they are present in the workplace. They also realize people have a life outside the workplace. How much do you know about the life of your follower outside the workplace? Privacy respected, many people perform better or worse in the workplace as a result of what goes on outside the workplace. Is your follower involved in community activities or their local church? Does she come from a large or socially active family? Is she a weekend athlete? Is he attending night classes? Is there illness in her family?

While a successful leader may never mention these factors directly, they still directly affect the business-related success of the follower. A wise leader would never ask the company courier (who happens to be a Deacon of the local Baptist Church) to run by the liquor store to pick up a bottle of scotch to have on hand for the visiting dignitaries from corporate headquarters. While the man may value his job, a task he is morally opposed to results in an erosion of commitment to all his other duties. On more than one occasion, a company has lost a great employee because the employee has been asked to be a part of something with which he has a problem. Sometimes, the employee quietly leaves the company without anyone knowing exactly what it was that caused him to go.

Sooner or later, we all tend to look out for our own best interests. We love our families, so we work hard to provide for them. We feel valuable and we want the finer things in life, so we want to be paid the highest dollar possible for our contribution to the company. With each passing year, we want to focus on the joys of life rather than the fearful downside of an unsure future. One reason we select our career and our company is that we are thinking ahead. Task by task, we do our best. Nobody wants to be labeled a "slacker". But if we see ourselves as vital to the mission of our company, we seem to *manufacture* energy and creativity. Simple, isn't it! Allow your people to perform within the areas they love and where they are best suited to excel.

Questions Get Results

One of the management basics involves control. In today's culture, we avoid controllers. But in management, control is essential. Show me an organization where the leader has lost control, and I'll show you an opportunity for a new leader to take over. The term "manage" involves the control of efforts and activities. How do you get your people committed to your company's objectives? How can you make sure they'll think like company people, and not simply wait for you to give out the daily activity list?

Remember the sales professional! You won't spend much time with a sales person before he asks you a question or two.

Actually, truly effective salespeople spend the first 25 to 30 % of the sales process asking questions and carefully listening to the answers. During this process, an interesting thing takes place. You begin to think about the subject of the questions. You begin to think about the product, as it relates to you and your family. The question, "How will the product be used?" causes you mentally USE the product! You are mentally creating a need for the product by thinking of the answer to the questions the salesperson asks.

Remember your parents! When your first upset came with the family car, there was a question in your mind, "What am I going to tell my folks?" You were mentally answering to them as you formulated the story.

Remember your teachers! You didn't pass the course until you had answered the questions! In class, you did your very best to focus on the words of instruction so you'd be able to answer the questions.

As you conduct your daily business, are you asking questions or are you making statements? Questions cause all listeners present to mentally formulate an answer. If all those hearing your questions are thinking of answers, then YOU are in charge of the thought process of all those people. On the other hand, your *statements* may be met with questions in the minds of those same listeners. Are you brave enough to ask your follower, "How would YOU do this", then to sit quietly and listen to the detailed answer? Can you see yourself asking follow-up questions about each detail of the answer your employee gives? Amazing, isn't it! Want to gain control of your organization? Become the person who asks the genuine, thought provoking questions! And LISTEN to people!

Great Leaders Know The Options

Wise leaders are masters at emotionally involving their people in the achievement of company goals and objectives. All our lives, we've made choices, based upon the options available. Once we made our final choice, we mentally *owned* the decision. Ask me to perform a task for you that you have initiated, in a manner you have carefully explained, and I'll do almost exactly what you instruct me to do. But if I choose a particular task from several other tasks and I choose an exact method of accomplishing that task, it has become MY pet project. Now I'll give it my all! Reporters have been responsible for selling millions of publications for a large publishing company because they have pursued *their story* aggressively. No manager needs to motivate them or threaten them with deadlines. The passion of the employee *on a mission* far surpasses any drummed up motivation coming from the boss. These followers see their superiors as *enabling their success* in the workplace, rather than ordering them around. While it is the leader's role to make the final decision, followers are given the option of following plan A or plan B.

Think of it, what options have you been making available to your employees lately? "Do this <u>or else</u>", "My way <u>or the highway</u>"? Go back in your mind to those days when you were on the lowest rung of the ladder. You've risen to your current level of success by becoming an in-charge sort of person. There's a *little* of that in your weakest follower, and a *lot* in your most valuable follower. You'll never know it's there until you open the avenue of choice to them.

Great leaders, like successful salespeople, make their success look easy. They are upbeat, possibility thinkers! Their followers enjoy working for them and feel vital to the company mission. Employees are just as committed in the absence of the boss as when the boss is in the same room. On those rare occasions when followers are despondent over a project or some market situation, great leaders help them regain their focus. They inspire followers with their genuine concern for them. Followers are fiercely loyal to great leaders, like customers are loyal to successful salespeople.

It's possible to buy a great leader's employee away from that company, but you'd better bring a lot of money to the table!

Minding the store

Chapter three

It's All In Your Mind

Near the little town of Hertford North Carolina is a community named New Hope. New Hope is steadily becoming a thriving place. Each week, someone moves a new doublewide in or starts building a home. People are retiring there and starting families there. New Hope is a happening place.

In the early 1950's, things were different in New Hope. It was sparsely populated with farmers who didn't just SAY they were poor, they were poor. Folks had outdoor toilets that used to "blow over" during a Hurricane. Every back yard was the location for a water pump that you had to prime and a ladle for drinking from the pump, unless you wanted to block the water with your hand and drink it straight from the pump. Folks didn't have a garage to keep the car or truck in, they had a car shelter.

Sunday mornings, the man would back the car out of the shelter and pull up to the back door, where upon the woman would file the children out to the car and the family would head for church. Back in the early 1950's, church was an event in New Hope.

21

Everybody you knew was there! If a person didn't go to church, folks figured him for some sort of infidel and steered clear of him. You couldn't trust a man who didn't go to church.

In the summer, all the windows were open and your Granny kept both of you cool with one of those Funeral Home Fans that you had to crease to keep it from flopping in the middle. In the winter, both stoves were red hot and the place usually smelled of Mentholatum. On the wall was a sort of menu board with the numbers of the songs you were going to sing that Sunday. You'd look in the songbook to see if your favorite hymn was on the program. Church was where most folks learned to read music and sing it. Congregational singing involved all the parts. Mrs. Caddy behind you would be singing, "In the sweet" and old Mr. Eure down the bench from you would echo that bass refrain, "In the sweet" and the whole Church was full of people singing bass and tenor and alto and even some parts that sounded invented. There was no sound system, just an old upright piano that seemed twice as loud on your favorite song. The Sunday morning choir special was usually a hymn that was chock full of alto, tenor and bass. You'd tap your foot and at the end of the song, everybody would say, "Amen!" if it was a real winner. The preacher always seemed to have a sermon about something you'd never heard of even if you were 90 years old and had gone to Vacation Bible School every year. And it usually would be discussed over dinner. By the way, dinner was the meal that folks in New Hope ate at noon.

After Church, the men gathered outside and smoked…the children played tag…the teenagers courted and the women worked at getting everybody to the car so you could get home before dinner burned. Summer or winter, church was a part of life. It was the one common thread that ran through the lives of all the folks in New Hope. As a matter of fact, when any church had a revival, you went, homework or not, and the place was always packed.

Only a couple of affluent families had TV's. TV was NOT highly recommended by the preacher of the Berea Church of Christ, by the way. But every family had a front porch with a swing and 2 or 3 rocking chairs. On any given fair-weather Sunday afternoon, you'd take your family in the car, a Ford or a Chevrolet, and you'd ride out. "Riding Out" is a lost art. The man drives slowly (no faster than 20 MPH) and looks intently down each furrow of each field, along each road in the county. As he drives, he slowly waves to each approaching vehicle, occasionally stopping to visit with another who's "riding out".

Eventually, someone in the car spots a family on the porch and you stop to sit a spell. No one called ahead to see if it was OK to drop by. There were no appointments. You just turned in to the path that led up to the house. Visits were lengthy, too, usually involving a meal or at least some sweet tea. The best porch visits attracted 4 or 5 more carloads of people "riding out" and started to resemble a family reunion. Men smoked and talked about the crops. Women talked about children, recipes, their health and church. Children had the MOST fun. They climbed trees, played cars in the dirt under the house, drove pie plates around the yard, went in the house to see the resident kid's toys and always ended up sweaty, nasty and spanked. You'd hop back in the car in the nick of time to get home for a sponge bath before youth meeting and Sunday night church.

Sunday night church was always packed. People would sing louder than on Sunday morning and there would be an extra song or two. The piano actually sounded louder at night than on Sunday morning. The choir would sing the special from a hymnal, then the preacher would preach until all the old men and little children were asleep. His message was never monotonous. He'd shout to make a point, slam his fist on the Bible or the Pulpit, folks would say 'AMEN!' when he threw the truth out there. Children didn't sleep because it was boring. They just slept because they were worn out!

During the week, folks worked. In the summer, kids worked too. Of course, kids went to school during the winter, so they could only work two or three hours a day and all day Saturdays. After all, they had homework to do. If someone came to your house during the week, this was the sign of a crisis! Perhaps a death or everybody was pitching in to get some agricultural chore done (pick the crop, build the barn, fix the tractor).

Folks didn't waste their valuable time in New Hope back in the early 1950's. They worked. Folks weren't bored in New Hope back in the early 1950's. They were busy. Folks didn't give much thought to being poor in New Hope back in the early 1950's. After all, everybody was poor and "the love of money" was "the root of all evil". Folks just focused on the work during the week and the Lord on Sunday.

You may have never been to New Hope or even to North Carolina. Chances are, you're too young to remember the early 1950's. One thing is for certain, you have experienced what life was like in New Hope on a Sunday in the early 1950's. It's all in your mind!

What A Memory Bank!

Someday, your children or grandchildren will ask you what life was like when you were a little boy or little girl. You'll respond with word pictures similar to the ones you just read.

The mind is incredible! Years after an event in your life, you can recall intricate details of that event. Everything you've ever seen, heard, tasted, touched or smelled has left an indelible record in your mind. You may be thinking, "That's not the case when I study for a test or try to remember a client's name", but it IS!

Think of it, when you listen to a friend talk with you the words go through your auditory nerve to your brain. Each word your friend says is etched in your mind. Some of the mumbled words are unexciting and some of the phrases go in one ear and out the other, but it all goes in your ear and to your brain. If you hear a persuasive speaker, the emotional presentation and the careful choice of words cause the message to seem as though it was put together with you in mind. In it goes! Everything you hear goes into your mind.

When you stand on the corner of a busy street and see the cars pass by, your optic nerve feeds this information to your brain.

Each person in each car, the color of each car, the make and model of each car is sent through your amazing optic highway to your brain. As you stand there, an automobile just like the first one you owned drives by. The memories come back! For a second, you're on your first solo drive again. You remember the times you had in that car and feel happy that your parents don't know about them. Some of the cars are average, though and most of the people are so far removed from your world that you don't even notice them. Actually, you APPEAR not to notice them. In fact, you see each person in each car. Think of the last time you heard of some eyewitness providing the link necessary to solve a crime. Your eyes are amazing! They see more than you realize!

Sometimes, your eyes are bigger than your stomach! You've just finished a delightful meal with your friends. The evening is delightful and the conversation is flowing. The waiter comes to the table with the dessert tray. Of all the problems in the world, you are faced with making a choice between two of your favorite desserts! What do you do? In a flash, you and your Sweetheart decide to each order one of the dishes. You'll share...the best choice yet! What IS your favorite dessert? Think of it, now. Amazing, isn't it, you were already thinking of it. Your mind did that! When you ate the dessert, your taste buds sent a message to your brain. Your taste buds also send a message to your brain when you eat your cereal each morning, when you have a sandwich for lunch or even when you drink a glass of water! Your amazing mind drinks it all in!

The Impact Of Emotions

One of the unavoidable phases of growing up is that time in childhood when you learn the meaning of pain. Of course, you fell a lot when you were learning to walk and you probably had your share of pain as a toddler. The pain of being hurt and KNOWING you're hurt is both physical and emotional! Do you remember the most common cure for those scrapes and bruises during your childhood? It was your mother's kiss and encouraging hug! Maybe that explains the importance we place on kisses and hugs as adults. Show me a happy person and I'll show you a person who gets plenty of kisses and hugs. Show me an unhappy person and you know the rest of the story. Emotional touching is definitely important to you. Think of all the times you experience the sense of touch in a day's time. Waking up, pulling the covers back, walking to the bathroom, taking a shower, drying and primping, getting dressed, eating breakfast, all this touching takes place in the first hour of your day! We haven't even mentioned driving to work, using your keyboard, greeting your clients or going out in the rain! Your amazing brain feels it all!

There's more to the rain than the wet sensation, isn't there! There's just something about a shower, particularly in the spring or early summer, that smells uniquely wonderful! Is it the flowers, or the grass, the trees or just your imagination? You can SMELL rain! Old folks in New Hope say you can actually smell it before it falls! Rain isn't the only thing you've smelled in your life. The fragrance of particular colognes send you into orbit. How can you explain that? Who knows why coffee always smells better than it tastes (sort of like pipe smoke). On a winter morning in your town, can you smell the smoke of fireplaces? Of course! If you're in Richmond, you can smell the tobacco. In Morehead City, you can smell the ocean. In Fort Worth, you can smell the stock yards. Your brain gets a whiff of something, logs it in, and you can go there without leaving your house. Did you ever think of the woods when someone cleans the bath with one of those pine cleaners?

All this information is in your mind! Of course, some of the information in your mind is destined to STAY there. That's understandable, when you think of the many inputs to your mind each minute of each day. You're constantly seeing, hearing, tasting, touching and smelling. Some of the inputs are so routine, you barely notice them particularly if you're a man. What you do notice are those inputs that register high on the emotional scale (wonderful things, terrible things). You also begin to form a value system, based on mental inputs through one of the senses that occur over and over.

We all remember our first love. Why? Because it was so wonderful! She paid so much attention to you and treated you as though you knew everything! You could do no wrong! She was at your beckoned call! You'd spend hours just looking at each other. Do you remember the telephone conversations? They consisted of compliments and promises, oos and ahs, and they went on for hours! Perhaps the reason you remember your first love was because of the way it ended. You had given her your heart on a silver platter and she SMASHED it! She told you she "needed some space" and you found out the space was needed so she could slip a new fellow into her life. You remember the day she told you it was over, then walked away with her head held high (you felt like slicing it off!). You had been fooled and that hurt!

If the emotional impact of an adolescent love affair can cause it to be a memory you can recall at any time, why not apply that principle to the business world. For instance, why not go out of your way to emotionally impact your clients, your boss and your subordinates. As a matter of fact, why not go out of your way to emotionally impact your Sweetheart! If the theory works, people will remember you and they'll see you in a positive light. Remember, their minds are being bombarded each minute with inputs just like yours. If you give them more emotional impact than all the other sources they're exposed to, you will probably be remembered. If your input is a positive one, it follows that they will have positive thoughts of you and your part in their life!

So, what type of boss are you? Do you go out of your way to impact people positively or do you spend your day putting out fires, only speaking to subordinates in order to handle a problem. Remember, the mind doesn't differentiate between the person who caused the chaos and the person fixing the chaos. The mind just makes a note of who brought the chaos to you! Are you telling your employees good things about themselves? They like that if the good things are believable. When you deal with your clients, are you solving their problems or are you telling them yours? Some problems are very entertaining. Are yours? Are people repeating your whined lines to their friends to entertain them? Probably! Should you stop telling people all about your problems? Definitely!

In today's business environment, the successful people are the people who realize the vital role the mind plays in every station of the workplace from the sales office to the loading dock. Business people destined for great things always think carefully about the impact of their daily routine on their personal success.

The people you hold in high regard are those who have made you feel good. The people for whom you have little respect are those who make you feel bad. Which are you?

Most folks would rather not be the leader

Chapter four

The Top, Home of the Lonely Brave

It's tough being *different* in a society where conformity is so very important. Not the type of *different* that caused you to be picked on by the big kids in grade school because you wore glasses or didn't join in the reindeer games, but the type of *different* that caused you to listen up in class and always do your homework. Our world is driven by the need to conform!

We dress to conform. An entire generation of American males can be easily identified by the presence of their preferred uniform. Low trousers and a hat worn backward will identify a generation, just as distinctly as the pin-stripe suit, white starched shirt and wingtips. If Mr. Backward Hat sees one of his peers dressed in a suit, the offender is harassed until he conforms! Seen from a distance, we quickly identify a man as young or middle aged by his uniform. Women have their uniforms, as well. Polyester dresses are worn by one generation of ladies while fashionable slacks and jackets by another. Still another generation of women wouldn't be seen in any attire other than jeans. Even the tender hearts of women are hardened when they look at a peer who is over or under dressed. When you wish to speak to the manager of an organization, you look for the one who looks like a manager. You know, the one not in uniform.

We socialize to conform. Perhaps you don't, but some social climbers actually vacation in the *correct* location. If their children want to go to that big theme park in Florida and everyone's going to Hilton Head this year, the kids are just going to have to understand! They have a boat, because everyone else has a boat. It may remain parked for the majority of the year, but when the boat owner roll call is read, they can answer, "35 footer"! They play certain sports for leisure because it's the socially acceptable thing to do. Who cares if the investment required in order to play the game is not commensurate with the degree of relaxation! Everybody else is a member there! They even attend the socially acceptable church! Don't ask them if they feel God has led them to that church unless you want to be called a Holy Roller. During the holidays, they carefully edit their greeting card list to ensure the right names are included. Parties are attended or avoided based upon the social strength of the groups giving and attending the events. If their name is omitted from an influential party for the first class people of their world, they may even manipulate their name onto the list! Even in selecting friends, today's up-and-coming are careful to make sure potential associates are socially OK. We certainly wouldn't want to suck up to the wrong group!

Is it any wonder, then, that we conform in the workplace! In all of our activities, we're busy becoming like everyone else. We certainly wouldn't want to be different at work! Being different in the workplace causes too much attention to be drawn to you. After all, they have names for the people who're always accomplishing great things and pleasing management!

One reason we aren't comfortable with being different is the great deal of courage required. Certainly, the people at the top are different. After all, they're management! They're the company people! You expect them to be different from the rank-and-file employees. Seldom are management types remembered as lowly beginners working their way to the top.

The rest of us are simply trying to hold on to our jobs, or ARE we? Many companies seem to have an <u>us against them</u> mindset between management and employees. Is this because there's a genuine difference in the two groups of people or is it because we're simply not brave enough to do our best, when our peers are just coasting? You may have heard the "I'll be more committed when I get into management", rationale. Sadly, we DON'T become more committed after establishing a character as a slacker. Do you know a slack manager?

What we're talking about is a life habit, or a part of our character. If your parents instilled in you the principles of always doing your best and being honest, respecting your elders and those in places of authority, if they established good habits like doing all your homework and going to Sunday School and church, if you were brought up to believe God was always with you even when other people weren't, then you're probably the type of person committed to excellence in the workplace. Your parents had an *impact* on your uniqueness. On the other hand, you may be someone who decided later in life to make the best of your opportunities, on your own. In either case, you made a personal decision to be different from the other people surrounding you. That took courage!

Success in this life involves a choice, not chance. People experiencing sudden unearned wealth seem to return to the financial place they were in life, sooner or later, especially those who see themselves as poor. Lottery winners, as well as those who inherit a fortune, often go through their winnings in record time. Of course, some are different. In the same way, a person who isn't driven to excel may actually find themselves catapulted to management, but it never lasts. Through an unfortunate series of events, they quickly adjust their life back to its destined boundaries. People who simply want to get by fail to succeed, even when given incredible opportunities, because they see themselves as strugglers. But the person who is driven to excel always has hope, no matter what his bank account balance is, and he always succeeds. He possesses the courage to press on, even at the risk of being labeled as different.

Driven people are driven <u>intentionally</u>! They begin each day with a specific outcome in mind. Before they even leave the breakfast table, many of them have a specific task or project in their minds. They go over it and explore all the possible avenues of accomplishment as they drink their morning cup of coffee. They arrive at the office and work from a list. Some make the list in the evening just before leaving the office, some do so first thing in the morning. Either way, they're always working toward written objectives. You'll never hear one of these great ones exclaim, "Let's go down to work and see what happens". They KNOW what's happening and what will happen. They planned it that way!

Their lives follow that pattern, as well. Great people plan their vocations and even their vacations! Their objectives include goals for this week, this month, this year and the years to come. Each goal or objective is written down in detail just like the daily list. When they plan to go on a vacation, their family can buy clothes and make reservations because it WILL happen. Have you missed a vacation lately due to poor financial planning or because your boss coerced you into skipping it until things got better. Don't feel bad if you did! Too many people do this every day.

Do you Suffer From Mental Malnutrition?

All this planning is just one of the habits successful people possess because they have taken time to force-feed their minds. So many folks talk about feeding your mind as though it's an option. It isn't! Your mind is being fed all day, every day. Everything you see, hear, taste, touch and smell feeds information into your mind. Most people are content to stand in line and take whatever the Mess Sergeant of Life dishes out. Sounds like an insult, doesn't it? It is! But it's true, never the less.

Most people give little thought to controlling the information entering their minds. They listen to whatever comes out of the radio or they watch whatever's on TV. When a pointless conversation occurs, they give no thought to moving from the area where the unproductive talk is taking place. In all these situations, people actually think they're NOT affected by second-hand information. They actually think they can be exposed to negative, or even damaging, information and it will have no direct effect on them since they weren't paying attention.

Do you realize that even when you DO pay attention to information, several repeated inputs are necessary for you to retain as much as 16% of what you were exposed to? If that's the case, maybe they're right! In a previous chapter, you read about your mind's ability to capture every event of your life. Focus on that fact for just a moment, in light of negative and damaging information.

Much has been written and said about the music and movies of our culture. People are generally convinced that too much of a bad thing will eventually effect your outlook on life. As a result, most folks are careful NOT to paint Satanic symbols on their small children's bedroom walls, NOT to listen to certain songs backward and NOT to watch Vampire movies just before bedtime. Any clear thinking person understands that doing these things will eventually bring about a result you don't want. If exposing a child to damaging symbols will eventually effect their value system, you have to agree that exposing your mind to information will cause you to think, act and talk in a particular way. Clearly stated, you become programmed by the information you see, hear, taste, touch and smell.

That's the difference in your body and your mind. You can't possibly accidentally feed your body. Food must be intentionally put in your mouth and chewed. It would be pretty hard for your enemies to sneak in your house and force food in your mouth when you weren't paying attention. Not so with your mind! Your enemies put garbage in your mind all the time with little comments you can barely hear. The comments don't even have to be about you or your loved ones to be damaging to your success. Hearing negative conversations in the workplace causes us to have negative information in our mental files. When you must draw from your files regarding a certain subject or issue, your mind doesn't know the difference in true & false, right & wrong, fair & unfair or reasonable & unreasonable. All your mind knows is the program. And your powerful mind sends the program through your mouth and down your silver tongue to the ears of your listener.

Great leaders are careful about what enters their minds. They begin each day with a healthy mental force-feeding of beneficial information. Certain people that you know, and possibly even work with, are successful today because they took time each morning for months to force-feed their mind. Some days, it's technique. Some days, it's theory. Some days, it's positive thinking. Some days, it's inspiration. Whatever it is, it always happens during the first half hour or hour of the day. Even though they aren't technically on duty until they reach their workplace, these great ones spend the first moments of their day in quiet mental force-feeding. Realizing the day will go downhill they choose to start at a high mental place.

Certain Things Make Me Mad, That's Just Me!

Your day may even go so far downhill that it will become a bad day. It's only human to have a bad day! You know the situation, perhaps personally! On bad days, we humans blow our tops! Everybody has an imaginary 'line in the sand'. Those crossing that line are in danger, especially when we're having a bad day! The receptionist is instructed, "Keep people out of my office, I'm having a bad day!" Those working in our area of the workplace retreat a safe distance when we're having a bad day. Even our family gives us plenty of room on our bad day. If, during a bad day, we sound off in someone's face, they seem to understand. They may even say, "I'll let this slide because I know you're having a bad day". They may SAY that, but what are they thinking? Could they be thinking, "*You've used your bad day to make MY day into a bad one! Just you wait until I get a chance to get even with you! Then you'll REALLY have a bad day!*"

My father often told me the story of a supervisor in the machine shop where he worked back in the 1930's who would routinely get mad and throw things. All day, each day, every employee of the machine shop was careful to avoid making the supervisor's life uncomfortable or difficult in any way. Sooner or later, though, he'd slip into one of his seething fits. He'd sometimes empty his toolbox and throw tools all over the shop when something made him angry. After a few minutes, he'd cool down. Then, in a pleasant voice, he'd apologize and instruct the crew to pick his tools up and put things back in order. Dad said he didn't remember much about that job but he DID remember the day that supervisor got fired. What a relief! Now the crew could focus on their work without feeling like they were on eggshells! Do you think productivity went up in that department? Do you think safety took a giant leap forward?

Certain events in this life will trigger your embarrassment and anger. Did you ever fall financially behind? That's so embarrassing and frustrating! More than anything, you wish to pay what you owe, but the debt seems overwhelming. Also overwhelming are the calls from the collectors. They can be very intense and intimidating! Sooner or later, the conversation escalates to loud threats and insults. Of course, collectors must be tough and persistent or they'll never scare you into paying, right? I thought that for years, until I overheard a conversation at a gathering one evening. Some ladies were talking about their careers and one of them happened to be an account manager for a large corporation. She explained to the other ladies that most of what she did was to collect overdue corporate accounts, some of them into hundreds of thousands of dollars. "Don't people get angry with you and tell you off", they asked, "What do you do"? A soft-spoken person by nature, she replied, "The meaner they become, the nicer I become. There's no need to answer anger with anger, especially when all you want is for them to write the check". She proudly shared with her friends that she had the highest percentage of funds collected, and the lowest percentage of overdue accounts in her corporation. Imagine having a job like that! All day long, you call people who've been called by OTHER creditors all day long and ask, "When can you pay". Do you think you might encounter a bulldog or two? How would you respond if someone who clearly owed you over a hundred thousand dollars started screaming at you? How many overdue accounts could you collect? On the other hand, if you'd been threatened by collectors all day and you received a call from a courteous sweet voice asking, "When can you pay", would you be more likely to discuss the situation in civil tones and perhaps even send a check?

Experiencing anger is a human weakness. If you're reading this and you've never been angry in your life, we need to talk. I'll document it and we'll BOTH be rich! The wise person simply sees this emotion as another human weakness that needs to be held in check. In Sunday School, you learned to "be angry and sin not". There's a mouth full! Be angry, go ahead! You're going to encounter those people and events in life that rub you the wrong way. When you do, that churning feeling inside you is natural and normal. You're angry and that's OK! But, be angry and sin not! You know the sins here; slander, theft, assault, even murder! If you THINK some terrible retaliation on the offender, it's easy to repent later after you have cooled down. On the other hand, if you DO some terrible thing <u>you</u> immediately become the offender! Think of anger as having a problem. The last person to ACT on the problem owns the problem. When you've been offended by someone, they own the problem unless you react to that offense. Then YOU become the owner of the problem.

Profanity—Official Language Of The Confused

One typical reaction of angry people is the use of profanity. I recall a military supervisor who used to explode a string of powerful profanities on us when things didn't go his way. We'd all quietly listen to our reprimand then try to do better. On one occasion, the words were very personal and involved slanderous implications about my heritage. It seems the sergeant thought my mother was a dog! Since I was young and brave and didn't understand the term, "insubordination", I felt the sergeant needed to be set straight. Some hours later, when he had cooled down, I respectfully told him she wasn't a dog and that she was very precious to me. While I understood that I had disappointed him personally, I wished he wouldn't hold it against my mother. He took a deep breath, put his hand on my shoulder and sincerely told me it *didn't mean anything*. I couldn't help wondering after that incident, "What ELSE does he say that *doesn't mean anything*". Profanity mixes people up! Regional slang that is complimentary in one part of the world is a strong insult in another. I like what one fellow named James said, "Let your *yes* be yes and your *no* be no". No need to mix people up with a lot of talk that sometimes involves physical impossibility!

Of course, using plain English when everyone about you is using profanity and regional slang, requires courage because it makes you different. One thing is for certain, nobody will ever wonder whether you mean what you say.

Eat, Drink And Be Humiliated

Life does involve bad days, tough people, company objectives and irate customers. It also involves times of celebration and relaxation. On all these occasions, drinking alcohol or adult beverages is a part of the landscape. Funny, isn't it, we refer to something that makes us act childish as an adult beverage! We Americans do love our alcohol, though. Some groups love alcohol so much that saying no to their offer of a toddy takes a great deal of courage! They look at you as though you've insulted them deeply! Far beyond taking a stand on morality or health on such an occasion is the importance of maintaining control of our wits. Even after an ounce of 3.2% beer, your body is adversely affected by alcohol. You may not smell, look, talk or walk like someone under the influence of alcohol. Sadly, you're under the influence. And, for some reason, alcohol works like a sponge! The more you drink, the more you want! Try arriving late at a party where alcohol is being consumed. Before you begin drinking alcohol, circulate and engage people in random conversation. Observe what they say and how they act. And who can forget that particular party where "old so-and-so" was 'loaded'! Remember how they thought they were 'fine', even as they made a complete idiot of themselves?

Imagine you're about to run the Boston Marathon. For months, you've prepared for this half-day race. You started a year ago by running 4 miles each day. Then you moved it up to 6 miles a day a few months ago. Last month and the month before, you even ran the full 26 miles. You went on line and checked your 26-mile time to make sure you were in the top of your age group. All year you've carefully selected your diet, making sure that you have eaten only the most nutritious foods, and in moderation! You've made it a point to get plenty of rest, especially during the month just prior to the race. Now the big day is here and you're ready for the race. The runners look like spectators, there are so many of them! Everyone is excited and ready for the opening gun to sound. Just before you take your mark, you remove your shoes and put several pebbles in each one. After all, you've walked with a pebble in your shoe before and you did fine! This is a special occasion, so you feel justified in having a lot of pebbles! How long would you last? A mile? Two miles? How long would it take to heal your feet? A month? Meanwhile, the Boston Marathon goes on and you've missed it for this year.

Before you think I've lost my mind with such an example, think of the results of consuming alcoholic beverages with company people or with customers. Like the marathon runner, you've invested time and sweat in your career. Additionally, It may have taken forever to win some of your clients and your team of followers over. It may have taken even longer for your boss to realize what an asset you are! Yet it can all go down the tubes in one conversation when alcohol is a factor, even if you're not the one doing the drinking! We all know alcohol impairs our ability to reason.

If you consume alcohol, don't do it with your business associates! You are where you are in the management chain because you are perceived as wise, sharp and organized. When you consume the smallest amount of alcohol, you fall under its influence. Even if you're only effected to a small degree, remember how you would feel if you were to detect alcohol on the breath of your dentist or your airline pilot. Business is business, even at a party! Alcohol is poison, especially with business associates.

Reading back over this chapter may cause you to think I'm a little old fashioned or some sort of religious fanatic. While that may or may not be true, neither factor is the reason I've recommended these concepts to you. You're the successful person you are because of your degree of uniqueness. There's something very special about you and about the way you do business. Others may have tried to imitate or duplicate your traits, but you're still the one who does what you do best.

You're <u>different</u>. You're a person of true courage!

So, how do you get them to work?

Chapter five

Building a Great Person, Beginning With You

One of the wonderful benefits of being an American is the luxurious standard of living we all enjoy. We still live in the wealthiest country on the face of the earth and have more freedoms than our global neighbors. I once read that individual Americans lose more money per year than most individual people in the world earn per year. If you've ever traveled to a third world country, you already know what a luxury your American lifestyle is.

Surrounded by all this affluence and living in this free society, we establish certain guidelines for what is, and what is not, acceptable for our day-to-day life. "I deserve" is a line heard daily in our country. "I deserve to be treated better than this", "I deserve a new car", "I deserve a vacation", and "I deserve a raise". Even the fast food industry feels you "deserve a break today". When we're reprimanded for our driving, our work habits or some other infraction, we often respond with "I didn't deserve that".

We all want to do as well as we feel we deserve to do. Human Behavior studies have shown that we seldom do *better* than we feel we deserve and, while we may temporarily operate *below* our level of what we feel we deserve, we eventually adjust our circumstances to where they deserve to be.

Even people who seem to always be down on their luck appear to feel as though they deserve that situation. Ever hear someone talk about how rotten his or her luck always seems to be? That's their way of admitting they are a rotten luck sort of person, in their own humble opinion. No matter what wonderful and exciting things happen in their life, they'll find a way to resume their downtrodden profile. In their mind, that's what they deserve.

At the same time, there is a minimum acceptable standard in your life. As a child, you probably played a sport that was your favorite. If you excelled at that sport, you wouldn't settle for some insignificant place on the team. After all, you were an expert and an expert deserves to be in a vital role! So it is in life. We seldom rise to leadership in a competitive organization until we feel we deserve that role. Most of the time, we reach that station in life long after we have come to the realization that we should be there. You may have been driven for years by your goal to lead an organization, wondering all the while why management couldn't take a hint and promote you. Once you reached the level you felt you deserved, you may have even set enviable performance records. You did so because you saw yourself as the type of person who does those things. Just like the person with the rotten luck, you adjusted your life to conform to your vision of what you deserve and who you are. We form this vision, or this level of self-confidence, based on the information in our mind. Most of that information is about you; it isn't simply general information that could pertain to anybody in the world. We tell others a little of this information each time we say things like, "That's the sort of person I am" or "Here's what I think". If someone listens to us long enough, we'll tell exactly who we are and what makes us tick.

Self-worth Is Not Self Determined

Strangely, our self-opinion is formed by the information put into our mind by those with whom we come in contact. When someone treats you with mistrust, a small "I'm sneaky and bear watching" deposit is made to your self-opinion bank. When a person gives you honor or respect, a small "I'm trustworthy and wise" deposit is made to the same account. Management puts you in charge of a project, resulting in a small "they're counting on me to deliver" deposit in that account. Ask any banker, and he'll tell you withdrawals can never exceed deposits. What others tell us about us tends to be who we become. There are exceptions, but the words said to you, about you, by your associates, mold the opinion you begin to form about yourself.

Who are you banking with? Your spouse tells you what sort of spouse you are, your children tell you what sort of parent you are, your boss tells you what sort of employee you are, your subordinates tell you what sort of leader you are. These are constants! You are a part of your family and you need your job. Therefore, you are faced with having to live with the things these people say to you about you. You're banking with others, though. The people you ride to work with, the people you have lunch with, the people you party with, the people you go shopping with all have an impact on your opinion of yourself. What deposits are you exposing your mind to on a daily basis? Are you carefully choosing your associates? You should! They're helping you decide how smart, successful, pleasant and attractive you are. All that is determining just how well you are doing in your life's pursuits.

Great Leaders Always Spread The Joy

Second only to our wish to do well is our wish for our friends to do well. We truly want our friends to be healthy and wealthy. It's a human trait, I suppose. Of course, that sentiment is limited to our friends. We don't wish any harm to the rest of the world; we simply aren't concerned with their well-being like we are for our friends' and ours. This is, unless we are the type of great person who has contagious confidence.

A friend of mine has contagious confidence. He has done very well in the marine industry. His product is expensive and in demand. As clearly as I can tell, he makes a nice profit on each sale and his company is making sales each day. He has dealers and customers all over the United States.

Since I'm a salesman at heart, my first reasoning about his success is that he has an aggressive sales force. Certainly, someone's out there beating the bushes for prospects, following up with the prospects and closing sales. After all, nothing happens until someone sells something. Right? Sure enough, his sales force works hard, but there's more to the story.

Actually, his success roots go deeper than prospect lists and power closes. His success stems from an attitude of confidence. It starts in his engineering department, goes through his factory, permeates his sales force and is extended to his customers. He's so committed to the success of other people that he even wishes for strangers to do well.

My friend is the sort of fellow who doesn't sponsor failures. In our community, you always feel better if he is involved in some undertaking with you. It's a sure sign of success! He's a happy man who always seems like he can't wait to do whatever it is he has decided to do that day. A man who has literally come up through the ranks by his own wit and drive, he works hard and is committed to whatever he does. Whether raising money to fight Cancer, leading a building project for his church, helping a friend enjoy the spiritual blessing of a weekend Emmaus Walk or cooking for a picnic, if it's worth his time he does it with commitment and high energy. His enthusiasm reminds me of something I once heard the great speaker Cavett Robert say, "I A S M in enthusiasm means I AM SOLD MYSELF". My friend's energy, commitment and enthusiasm are so contagious that you can't help feeling a little of it yourself, no matter the project.

That's the way he approaches the marine industry. He truly believes his product is unique and of high quality. He carefully chose to produce a product that addresses a specific need in the marine market. Naturally, when he markets that product, he does so without reservation! I've always thought his sales force has the easiest job on earth!

He listens to his potential clients and designs a product that will address their needs and concerns. For instance, another friend of mine once told me he'd rather have an outboard than inboard boat for deep-sea fishing. That seemed interesting to me! Why would you want a boat with the engines hanging off the stern like some sort of little bass boat? Why not have an inboard so you'd have cleaner lines? Then my friend told me he sometimes likes to fish 75 or 100 miles off shore. "If you lose your inboard engine, all you can do is hope your radio is working and wait for the Coast Guard to tow you home", he explained. My boat-building friend heard people talk about this too! He went to the drawing board with his engineering staff and designed a line of deep-sea fishing boats with redundant (twin) inboard engines. You may think this just drove the price up on the craft. Couldn't you save money by putting outboard engines on the boat? But that's the point; the customer prefers a clean stern while also having the peace of mind of twin engines. Seems like a simple thing. Listen to your customer and give him what he wants. How many manufacturers do that, though?

If his customer is important to him, so is his factory employee. On a tour of the boat factory, one would think he was just one of the guys who works there. You don't hear the "I" word come out of his mouth very much. Matter of fact, he constantly tells you how important every person at the factory is. "We've been blessed with really great people", he told me as we walked along. As we entered each particular section of the factory, every employee was busy. While nobody was goofing off, it was also noticeable that nobody stopped his or her work to politic with the boss. They were all far too busy doing important things! My friend explained each person's particular function and how vital to the process of building the boats each individual was. Another noteworthy fact in our tour was that each of the countless employees had a NAME. He referred to them, by name, and told about each phase of building their product as though that particular phase was the most important. He explained they had a flexible work schedule so a person in the factory could use the best 40 hours of the week to do their part in the timely construction of this fine product.

Think of it, only important people work at that factory! They all perform only important tasks! And they are all so important that they are primarily responsible to themselves for their own progress. While most employers are concerned with monitoring and micro-managing their employees to make sure they do their part exactly as they are told, here's a fellow who empowers and enables his employees! No wonder they produce such a superior product!   How many manufacturers display THAT type of confidence in their workforce?

Building this sort of self-confidence in the team results in less employee absence and fewer relationship type problems in the workplace. If you're a supervisor, you've certainly dealt with one of these issues this month! Employees who see themselves as vital usually think twice before they miss a day of work. They also relate well with others in the workplace since they don't feel threatened, and because they see others as vital employees as well. The product tends to be of a higher quality because of the degree of commitment of those building it. When an employee is called upon to defend the product, they do so with confidence and patience. Irate customers are seen as simply uninformed, and the employee confidently and politely informs the customer when problems arise. If your company is dealing with confrontational issues between customers and staff, the answer may not be a Complaints Department. Maybe what you need is a little more confidence among employees.

Their degree of self-confidence is built, much like your own, by the daily input of information about themselves. Do you tell the people working with and working for you when they're doing a good job? Do you rave about their great accomplishments? Do you make a big deal of the Employee of the Month award? These valuable compliments cause your peers and subordinates to raise their level of self-expectancy, especially when compliments are perceived as genuine. People rarely exceed your spoken expectations. What sorts of verbal input are you giving those around you?

Sometimes You Must Be The Drill Sergeant

None of us live in a perfect world, even in the good old USA. The task some managers most dislike is that of having to tell an employee their work or their work habits missed the mark. Have you seen the boss evade an issue with a person doing sub-standard work? I know I have! Sometimes it goes on for months, until eventually some crisis forces the issue to be dealt with. Usually this climate leads to over-reaction when the issue is finally brought to the surface. This happens because we humans dislike confrontation of all types.

I like it when people tell me I'm smart, witty and a good employee. I'll listen to this type of talk all day long. When the boss tells me I'm NOT, I begin to dislike the boss and question just how smart HE is. Does this sound like someone working for you? Does this sound like YOU? Now you see why people don't discipline their followers. It isn't very popular, and we all want to be liked!

One reason you were chosen to lead in your organization is your ability to tell people what it is they don't want to hear. If you can deliver bad news and have people listen, you are definitely management material. Great leaders must tell people when they are missing the mark. How else will they improve without knowing a problem exists?

Some employees actually produce below the level of acceptable performance because they don't realize they're doing it. They honestly think their work is OK! After all, nobody has said anything to indicate differently! When this employee's work is criticized, a tender approach is necessary. Otherwise, they can easily become offended and give up. If you hired this employee based upon their ability to do what was necessary, a friendly and practical "here's how to do better" often solves the problem. Realizing he can achieve greater things by accomplishing his current duties correctly often motivates this person. Such a person may have done a 75% job for so long that they may respond more favorably by having 100% introduced to them as a new concept. Remember, this is the conscientious employee who just isn't meeting the standard. Far too many leaders jettison this type of employee, reasoning they are *too far-gone* to be salvaged. You can train people all day long, but you can't buy commitment. This type of employee is committed. He simply needs the proper training.

Have you met the slacker? You know the type, never does what you expect unless he knows you're going to inspect. He always arrives at the last minute and is the first out the door at lunch and at quitting time. His idea of commitment is, "I want the company committed to my likes, dislikes, plans and ambitions". The first time the company requires something extra such as overtime, additional duties, or even 40 hours work for 40 hours pay, he's likely to bail out.

Realizing his lack of company spirit, this employee still becomes more vital and motivated when approached with a bit of positive leadership. Most uncommitted employees are that type because they don't see their job as a means of fulfilling their personal needs or goals. Once you listen to this employee enough, you begin to realize just what it is that motivates him. For some, it's recognition. He likes to have his name out there! For others, it may be the advancement. He wants to climb the ladder of success until one day he's the boss. Whatever the self-serving force that drives him, if you can identify it and tailor your comments to show how each phase of that employee's task is bringing him closer to that goal, you'll suddenly have a committed employee.

Great leaders know their people. They know who's motivated and who's not. When they interview prospects for a position, they listen for the driving force in that person's life. Doesn't that make your leadership position sound like a sales position? It is! Just as a great salesperson sells what the customer wants and needs, a great leader sells followers on accomplishing tasks based upon what the <u>follower</u> gets when the task is done. Leaders who ask followers to do something for the company have a smaller success rate than leaders who give opportunity to followers to achieve some personal goal by accomplishing a company task. The task is accomplished with a different presentation to the person responsible for it's accomplishment.

In the midst of all this positive thinking, please don't think that I live in a bubble! It's a known fact that leaders spend most of their time correcting blunders made by followers and handling discipline. After all, that's why you're a leader. You aren't afraid to point out the shortfalls of your workforce.

Do you criticize with the eloquence of a Drill Sergeant? Can you make people feel about an inch tall? Rest assured, when you point out a blatant shortfall in your follower's performance, he knows in his heart that you are right. People don't like to be belittled, though. Our minds close up when an authority figure "starts in" on us, even when we know we are at fault.

I like to compare it to the people in the Emergency Room at your local Hospital. If you suffer a painful fall and cut your forehead open, you go to the ER as soon as possible. Once you've filled out all the necessary forms, you're rushed to a treatment room and examined. The Doctor may comment about the severity of the wound or ask you how it happened. Within minutes, the Doctor deadens the area around the wound and begins closing the wound with stitches. Perhaps you are given a prescription for medication to ease the pain or speed the healing. The Doctor then tells you how long it will take to heal and an appointment is set for the stitches to be removed. Not counting the time spent with paperwork or waiting your turn to receive treatment, this takes an hour or two at the most. But the healing can sometimes take weeks. During the healing time, someone from the Doctor's office may even call to ask about your progress. Finally the day comes to have the stitches removed.

The Doctor criticized positively, then recommended a course of action and followed up. Sound familiar? We, as leaders, should do the same. It certainly works better when you spend a moment or two clearly stating to a follower that a certain part of their performance is unacceptable, followed by hours or weeks of corrective training and follow-up. Unfortunately, many leaders do the opposite. They spend long periods of time dwelling on the shortfalls of a follower's performance. This is enough to make the average employee want to quit. If he stays, they tell him to shape up and do better. That's a lot like the Doctor looking at your bleeding forehead and saying, "You can't expect to be healthy with a gash in your forehead! Don't you know you could bleed to death? Think about what you did to get that gash and resolve yourself to never do that again!" He would be right in every statement he made. But that wouldn't close the hole in your forehead.

Are you mending wounds or expounding on the evils of bleeding? You're the leader! No employee is going to come to you and give you a course on effective criticism, especially if they are the one who needs criticism. Remember the bank account in their mind. If you put in good, they draw out good. If you tell them they have too much potential and they are too valuable to be performing below the standard, and then show them how to do whatever it is you need them to do, they are likely to listen. If you follow your brief criticism with interesting training and encouraging words, your follow-up inspection will reveal a productive employee.

Are You Ready For Hero Status?

One of the perks of leadership is being identified as the boss. Sooner or later, you'll be away from your work environment and run into one of your followers. They may introduce you to their friends by saying, "This is my boss". Look into their eyes. Do you see shame? Do you see resentment? Hopefully, you see admiration and loyalty.

The very fact that you are the leader requires you to always put your best foot forward. People are relying on you to make the tough decisions and deal with the pressures of leadership successfully. After all, that's why you are the leader and they are the followers. That's why you are paid more than they are. Great leaders avoid the very appearance of weakness and the human factor in the workplace. When a great leader has a problem, he discusses it with a professional who specializes in that area. Remember, as a leader you solve problems. Followers come to you with their problems for help and advice.

Many of your followers never give a thought to the situations you face in your own personal life. Have you ever had a personal problem exposed to your followers and found that very situation, which had nothing to do with your ability to function as a leader, affecting your ability to lead your people? The reason is simple; people find your problems entertaining and unusual. In so doing, they allow their focus to drift from business to entertainment. As a leader, you are highly visible. Your entire organization can mentally justify stopping their tasks to discuss your problems.

Do you have a problem with your car? See a mechanic. Are there problems in your marriage? Seek counseling with your Minister or a Marriage Counselor. Are financial problems clogging your mind? Talk with your Banker. Keep it out of the workplace. Your credibility is at stake. If people must know negative things about you, make them find them out on their own.

Focus on being a great person. Focus on being a Hero because, to someone, you are!

Crybabies and hot-heads

Chapter six

The Role Of Enforcer

As a leader in your organization, are you mission-oriented or are you people-oriented? Mission-oriented leaders strive to practice empathy, but they truly have to work at it. Empathy is pretty easily defined. It's the mindset that understands how a follower feels without agreeing with them.

Sympathy—Let's Not Hurt People's Feelings

Politicians practice <u>sympathy</u> rather than empathy. They say, "Let's take an opinion pole so I'll know what I think. Ask detailed questions so I'll know just how passionate I am about it." Many leaders, like politicians, are focused on being popular and being accepted. They can't make any decisions until they know what will be accepted by the rank-and-file. Growth never happens during their watch because they are too busy trying to please everybody. As you know, growth involves change from what we *know and like* to what is *new and different*. Of all things in this world, people resist change the most.

Practice sympathy with your child regarding his homework and you short-change him for life. Sometimes homework isn't fun. Sometimes it lasts until the wee hours of the morning! On those occasions, it's easy to remember how you felt when you were the one studying or working out those math problems. There's a part of a loving parent that wants to tell your child, "Go to bed! Forget that stuff! You'll never diagram sentences or identify the parts of a grasshopper once you enter the workforce!" But you know better. You know your child's momentary discomfort will pay off later in life.

The same applies to those who follow your lead in the workplace. Let them slide and the person paying the ultimate price will not be you or the company. As a goal oriented manager, you'll simply have another employee take up the slack. Your company may not grow due to the people-oriented management style, but at least it won't shrink. The person paying the highest price will ultimately be the slack employee! They'll be the unemployed or underemployed. If you truly feel for your followers, you'll take the time and invest the effort required to enforce standards and assure accomplishment of company objectives. Vince Lombardi, famous coach of the Green Bay Packers back in the late 1960's, told his followers there was no feeling like being completely exhausted on the field of victory. *Tired* successful employees, like *tired* successful leaders, are more fulfilled than completely rested slackers. Successful people feel the elation of victory and accomplishment. Those who aren't putting forth an honest effort feel the constant nagging of their guilty conscience.

Apathy—A Bull In A China Shop

The power-hungry, on the other hand, practice <u>apathy</u>. They focus on doing the exact opposite of what's expected, for the sake of being different. They say, "I have the power! I don't care about you, or even about the company objectives! I just want you to answer to me!" These corporate bullies are known for getting things done at the expense of others. They haven't had a successful day until someone has suffered a broken spirit at their hand.

Most of these self-oriented (another people-oriented type) leaders are determined to make a name for themselves. They honestly desire to set records and achieve unbelievable feats, in order that they may feel better about themselves. What they don't realize is that self-centered leadership alienates everyone.

They become proficient at firing people because, sooner or later, every person answering to them gets tired of dealing with a bully. The followers eventually muster enough courage or frustration to give the bully a piece of their mind, grounds for dismissal. Apathetic leaders have many rules and regulations. After all, that's part of their kit. They require followers to spend volumes of valuable man-hours generating pointless reports and spreadsheets. They are information intensive.

All this is a mere smokescreen for reminding people THEY have the power and THEY know best and THEY are in charge of every single decision. Apathetic leaders, given enough rope, eventually cause enough grief and loss of morale among the followers that they are fired. It's always nasty and sometimes comes too late.

Empathy - Getting The Job Done

Mission-oriented leaders enforce standards and accomplishment of company objectives. "I understand how you feel", can only be said after taking the time to sit quietly and listen. Sometimes, a follower expresses strong opposition to performing a particular task, accepting a new responsibility or even working with a particular individual. As a leader, you have the choice of forcing the issue or caving in and allowing the follower to assume the role of decision maker for your organization. Wise leaders pursue a third option. A wise leader will listen until he has a clear understanding of the follower's true feelings concerning the situation. Then, with a clear head and a friendly but firm manner, he will explain to the follower why this decision has been made and just how important the follower's role is. In other words, "I understand how you feel but I don't feel the same way. I'm responsible for accomplishing this task so we're going to do this the company way. I appreciate your support in the success of this task! "Frankly, the average person will go along with a leader that takes the time to hear their side of things and explain why the company is taking this tack, even if he disagrees.

Empathetic leaders also must fire people. It's never pleasant to look a person in the eye and say, "I'm taking away your ability to earn a living at this organization". But with the same commitment that a State Trooper shows when he issues his mother a traffic citation, great leaders must accomplish this task. That's why you were chosen for your leadership role. You have the backbone required to let someone go. Sometimes you like to do this, particularly when the person across the table has caused you many sleepless nights and isn't liked by anyone on the staff.

Most of the time, empathetic leaders hate to fire people. Great leaders seldom fire a person without notice. The follower is only called in for the bad news after several counseling sessions and intensive training. But when the decision is made that a personnel change must be made, the empathetic leader rises to the occasion. Sometimes, the person being fired is a nice guy. Many times this nice guy needs this job! If he isn't meeting company standards, he knows why he's being dismissed. He may have hard feelings for a short period of time, but in the long run his life becomes better and the company becomes stronger.

You'll really know you've met an empathetic leader when that leader recognizes or promotes an unpopular employee for doing an outstanding job. Popularity isn't vital to this leader! If a follower is disliked for whatever reason, the leader looks past that personality quirk to the accomplishment of company objectives. The Sales Manager tolerates unusually large egos in sales people when they produce outstanding revenue. Radio and Television Network executives overlook outlandish demands from staff when their shows bring huge numbers in the ratings.

As you read these words, are you wondering what your boss has overlooked in your personality?

Is this a popularity contest?

Chapter seven

Running in the right circles

Success on life's journey is a lot like the aging process. If you keep waking up each day and eating meals, you'll probably live a long time. Look around at the people in your community. Some have no nutrition and/or exercise plan at all, yet they're still alive. But if you exercise faithfully, if you eat the right foods moderately and if you keep a good outlook on life you'll not only live a long time, you'll actually enjoy it!

In the world of work, it's possible to successfully coast along. If you continue to show up at the same place each day and continue to do your best, you'll probably keep your job. If that weren't the case, there would be a lot more street people. But if you strive to learn everything you possibly can about your career, if you approach your work with a plan to succeed and if you treat your followers as the important people they are, you'll not only keep your job, you'll LOVE it!

Love Your Job

Do you love your job? Or are you going to work every day, even though you DON'T love your job, because you need the money? Don't feel guilty if you're involved in your career for the money. After all, many people in our society have selected careers or joined companies simply because the money was too good to pass up. Reality tells us we must go to work and earn a living. There are bills to pay and things to buy. Growing children have appetites and require new shoes. Beyond that, we Americans have expensive tastes and a competitive spirit that causes us to easily rationalize spending 40 to 60 hours each week doing something we don't like so that we and our families can spend the weekend or a vacation having fun. So we suffer along like a donkey striving to get an unreachable carrot on the end of a stick.

Wise old King Solomon wrote, "He who seeks silver will never be satisfied with silver". Perhaps he had witnessed those who had sold out for a paycheck. Like the donkey, we're only fooling ourselves if we think we'll ever reach some plane of fulfillment by spending our lives doing something we don't like. How can we ever hope to excel while doing something we can't put our heart into?

Think of the most successful and financially blessed person you know. I'm not speaking of someone who's making a good living, or of someone who was born with a silver spoon. Think of a RICH person, someone who has made his or her own way in this world and done very well. If you know them very well, visit them in their workplace. Observe how they do the little things and how they make the big decisions. Watch them interact with their followers and customers. They have chosen to do the job they love. If you love your job, your whole heart goes into every task. You don't focus on the money or how many sick days you have left. You're not obsessed with whether you have taken all your allotted breaks today. If you need to work an extra hour or two, you do so without even thinking twice. Even vacation and promotion, though they are important, take a back seat to the successful accomplishment of your daily tasks.

If it's Worthwhile, Give It Away

Successful leaders are givers, too! Early in life, they realize the value of helping others. Ask any person who has participated in a charitable project! When you give to someone, and that gift enhances the quality of life for that person, your reward is far greater than theirs. Ask a giver to spend an hour with an employee who needs some attention and the answer is yes. One of the oldest truths is that the teacher learns far more than the pupil. People who have invested their hearts into their careers are always eager to help others within the organization achieve their goals. Givers volunteer to address any need. They realize one can never give more than they have returned to them. Such a person becomes focused on contributing, rather than acquiring. When some undeserving person is promoted ahead of you, your giving spirit causes you to facilitate their success rather than complaining about the inequities of the system. It's possible that you realize your kind spirit will encourage that person to become a more motivated and committed employee.

Know Who's Who

Early in life, we all learn the pain that comes from impressing the wrong person. Have you ever impressed someone in a position of authority, only to have that person retire or transfer? Perhaps you've concentrated on impressing your loved ones by completely departing from your normal character and putting on your best behavior at some social or family function. The compliments fill the car on the ride home. Your family can't believe how remarkably you have behaved at the outing, but it backfires on you! Now, they expect you to act that way all the time!

Great leaders aren't interested in impressing anyone. As a matter of fact great leaders don't even <u>try</u> to impress people! The leader knows what's expected and is committed to doing his or her very best. Sometimes, people notice. More often than not, nobody is even aware of the contribution.

Are you finding yourself doing a lot of work that is going unnoticed? Congratulations! You posses one of the traits of great leadership - You're an anonymous success. Believers in God don't need a lot of "rah-rah" made about their accomplishments in the workplace. They know God is always watching them and His opinion is far more important that any fickle man's.

If you're doing your very best and if you feel you're doing what God would have you do, who's left to impress? Oddly enough, when you begin to think and act like this everyone is impressed. And everyone wants to follow you!

Surround Yourself With Mirrors

Special triple mirrors are conveniently located in clothing stores so you can examine your prospective purchase. Watch people trying on clothes in a store. They pose and move about to see just how the garment will hang on them. Will it make them look big? Is it well made? Does it fit their image? You've been in front of that mirror, haven't you! You've looked and decided to buy, or not to buy, based on how it made you look in the mirror.

Successful leaders realize that you become what you are exposed to. Ask yourself, "How will my friend's conduct look on me? Is his commitment to company goals and objectives reflective of the way I want to look? Speaking of looking, how about the way my friend dresses? And does my friend treat people with respect? Is his general conduct and language the type I want to copy?" Realize you WILL become like your friend if you spend enough time with him or her.

In Texas there's an old saying, "Lie down with Dogs and you'll get up with fleas!" That old saying has been proven time after time. Remember your college days, or your time spent away from home in the military. Remember being a member of a winning sports team. Remember your friends back in high school. You may not be like them now, but you were then.

Run with the tigers and you'll become a tiger, hang back with the lazy and you know the rest of the story. Choose your associates carefully. They're telling you who you are and they're setting standards for your life.

"Lucy, you got some 'splainin to do!"

Chapter eight

Go To The Head Of The Class!

On September 11, 2001, America was attacked on her own turf by terrorism in a magnitude unlike any imaginable. Even the painfully tragic Oklahoma City Federal Building bombing was small in comparison to the massive blow struck by terrorists in the damage to the Pentagon and the leveling of the World Trade Center in New York City. Most overwhelming to Americans was the sudden loss of so many innocent lives as the passengers of all those Airliners, the people working in those buildings and those trying so valiantly to rescue the trapped and injured suddenly lost their lives. Most of us realized the heroic acts of those passengers who overwhelmed their captors and plunged to their deaths in a field in Pennsylvania saving many lives in Washington DC. We took heart to know the enemy was partially deprived of a victory, but we were emotionally defeated for a brief moment in time as our world stood still.

For a brief time, Americans were lethargic. Consumed with the latest Television report on details of the tragedy and how it would touch our very lives, we were glued to screens and to talk radio.

Even at work, employees were blatant in their search for information on news websites rather than the timely accomplishment of the day's business goals and objectives. Stores tuned their televisions and radios to the reports. Salespeople stopped asking for orders. Most people simply wanted to spend time with loved ones or stay close to home. The business of governing the country came to a halt as members of the Congress and the Senate of the United States individually condemned the acts and promised retaliation for those who had perpetrated them. It seemed September 11th was to be the end of life as we knew it forever.

Then, a man went on TV and told us to go back to work, start shopping again and get on with life, assuring us he would take care of the details we were so concerned with. President George W Bush did what Winston Churchill did during the darkest hours of World War II. He communicated effectively. His communication was so effective that the patriotism and spiritual commitment of Americans reached an all-time high. Because of the way President Bush conducted himself and because of the words he said to Americans during the following months, his popularity was higher than any modern day US President's had been. All because he communicated effectively and accomplished what he said he would.

Interestingly, when President Bush ran for office and even after he was elected, one repeated criticism by his opponents and by most in the news media was that he was a poor communicator. They had decided he wasn't destined to be a successful leader, based on their own perception of his lack of communicative skills. They certainly judged President Bush as not possessing the gift of effective communication. They expressed shock and surprise as he delivered the inspiring words day after day that would strengthen, focus and rebuild the heart of Americans. Many believe the heart-felt passion of President Bush was the catalyst of his dynamic communication during this critical moment in our history.

Successful Communicators

Successful people are great communicators. There's no other way to put it! They simply have the knack for making their words simple and easy to apply. Long before they reach the ranks of leadership, they're known for being able to give the straight scoop on everything from instructions on the newest hardware in the marketplace to the story in a nutshell about the company's latest new policy. Unlike great statesmen or clergy, they never seem to need big eloquent phrases and they always seem to be able to say everything in 25 words or less.

Is the ability to communicate effectively a gift? Some believe it is. Some believe you're either a born speaker or you're not. Some are referred to as introverted or just quiet. Those who believe communication is a gift seldom call on these sorts of people to communicate information on behalf of the company. As a matter of fact, some are overlooked for promotion to management positions because they're perceived as too timid or not too well spoken. On the other hand, we all know cases where the opposite is the case. We can all call the name of a well-spoken person who is in over his managerial head. Who among us hasn't voted for a politician because we liked what he had to say or the way he said it, only to find that same politician wasn't listening to his own words! We all know someone who is a great communicator but who isn't proficient at the rest of the job.

No, effective communication isn't a gift. It's a skill. Like athletic skills or business skills and all other skills, the art of effective communication must be learned and practiced. Further, it must be adapted to fit the personality of each individual who would master it. And it must be delivered with heart-felt conviction.

That leads us to the other end of effective communication, the receiver of that information. Many leaders make the honest mistake of determining exactly what it is they wish to say, without giving much thought to the desired response. Whether a powerful electronic presentation or a speech filled with passion, they prepare their information in a corporate vacuum and present it with enough emotion to intimidate Zig Ziglar. When it falls on deaf ears, the speaker is amazed! How could this be? It was a great presentation! Why didn't ANYBODY get the point? Why aren't they motivated? In order for communication to be complete, it must be customized to the needs and comfort of the receiver.

Successful Communication is Intentional

Great Generals spend twice as long preparing for a battle as fighting it. Coaches train their teams of players in the basics of winning a sport for weeks, in order that a two-hour encounter with the opposing team will be successful. Effective communication is very similar. The successful communicator carefully plans each presentation. Even when a communicator is called upon to make a presentation 'on the spur of the moment', he follows a prescribed format. Winging it is a sure way for a communicator to crash!

The goal of communication is to transfer feeling from the sender to the receiver. For that reason, the effective communicator spends time getting to know the needs of the receiver. Who is the audience? What is the occasion? What is the goal of this presentation? What's important to these people? What do they already know about the subject I'll be addressing? How do they feel about the subject I'll be addressing? Do they know me? How do they feel about me?

In eastern North Carolina, we have a term called 'chasing rabbits'. The term describes a person who has begun to tell a story and, while using an example in the midst of relating the story, has changed the subject entirely until they are now telling the 'example' rather than the story. Research is a tricky word that sometimes sends people on a rabbit chase. Conscientious communicators have often spent hours researching information on line or in a library when they already have the information. The first place to go on a search for information relating to your presentation is to your own mind and your own life experiences. No one knows your experiences with the detail that you do. No one feels the passion you do about those things that have happened on your life journey. Start there. Ask yourself, "What do I know about this subject?" Perhaps the reason you're the person selected to make the presentation is because you are the expert in the opinion of the audience or of those in authority.

When writing your presentation, begin with the end. That's right! You would never leave your home on a business trip without having a definite destination and an idea of how to get there. Giving a presentation is a lot like taking a trip. First, you must know where you want to take your audience. Imagine you are invited to speak to your company's shareholders about why your department showed an unusually high expense in the past year. The expense in question is responsible for their not receiving a dividend check. You have been allocated 15 minutes in the annual meeting. You are prepared with a persuasive presentation that will put things into perspective. Emotions are high and all eyes are on you. At the last minute, the President of your company leans over and whispers to you, "The last speaker went 20 minutes over. Several of these shareholders have pressing commitments that cannot be overlooked or postponed. Twelve of them have hitched a ride on a neighboring company's corporate jet that will leave with or without them. You have five minutes." He's the boss! People are restless! They want to hear what you have to say, but they want you to say it quickly. The corporate jet will leave them. The facts are the facts! If you were told by the person leading the meeting to change the length of your presentation, could you? You could if you had written the ending first.

Preparing the end of your presentation FIRST means putting the entire presentation into a nutshell. A great speaker once said, "Tell 'em what you're going to tell 'em, tell 'em, then tell 'em what you told 'em". If that's the way you are prepared to present your material, ANY length of time is excellent. You can easily present an hour-long talk in 5 minutes! Simply go to the closing of that talk.

With the end of your presentation set in stone, next determine the MAIN POINTS of your presentation. The most effective presentations seem to be the ones with the least number of main points and the most interesting information to support those points. Information overload will quickly cause an audience to feel defeated in their effort to follow a speaker. Having too many main points in one's presentation causes all the information to go over the heads of the audience. Surprising enough, having too little support for the main points of a presentation causes the listener to miss the point entirely. Plainly put, keep the main points of the presentation to a minimum yet develop each main point to the nth degree! Great speakers tend to leave their audiences with 1 or 2 ideas after as much as an hour of talking! And the audience has it!

Finally, write the opening remarks of your presentation. What a novel approach! First, you write the end. Last, you write the BEGINNING! Experienced presenters will tell you they have changed their opening remarks as they stood up to address the audience! Opening remarks are designed to help engage your audience and gain their attention. They will make you feel at ease and they'll relax your audience. They will cause your audience to want to listen to your comments.

One of the great shocks of my life came when I discovered that many great people had professional writers on their staff. I thought all the great statesmen were like Abraham Lincoln. Certainly they sat down with a legal pad and wrote their own speeches out in longhand! As I grew up and saw people give speeches and make presentations, I realized some do better at writing and some do better at presenting. This philosophy won't work for the leader in today's marketplace! Not only must great leaders write information down effectively, they must convey that information to the listeners with equal expertise.

Stand and Deliver

Have you heard the adage that people would rather go to the dentist than give a speech? How is it in your organization? Do people argue over who will have the privilege of speaking at the next employee meeting or is the subject more like, "Who can we get to do it?" Many experienced speakers actually prefer to speak to a large group rather than to a single stranger. As with many types of fear, the fear of speaking before a group is based on one's lack of experience. In other words, we fear the unknown.

There is no deep dark secret to standing in front of a group and sharing some information successfully. With your presentation prepared and familiar, simply stand up and present it. The successful communicators in today's marketplace personalize their presentation, just as they have personalized their comments, with a presentation style that fits the occasion and audience.

One of the cardinal rules of professional speaking is don't allow your personal life to interfere with your duties on the stage. I remember the pain of knowing a presentation I was making was going down in flames. Because of some personal news I had received just prior to arriving at the auditorium where I was to speak, I was preoccupied with that bad news. I was giving a talk on a subject I was very familiar with, yet it just wouldn't come together. Even though I <u>knew</u> the audience was slipping away, my words wouldn't bring them back! That news that seemed so overwhelming was controlling my thought pattern. I was saying some of the same words I had said when I have given that talk on other occasions, but this time I had worry on my mind and all over my face! Being worried about the news had caused me not to smile and not to relax. My audience was just a tense as I was! Matter of fact, they seemed worse! The personalization I normally would have used for a group such as this was replaced with examples and comparisons of a person who had just experienced the news I had experienced. My audience had no idea why I was off on a tangent about that particular subject. They probably thought it was all part of the speech! If you've ever watched as a speaker has bombed, you know the feeling. You sit there in the audience wishing you could hold up a cue card or excuse the speaker from this awful moment! Sort of reminds one of the bad dream about being in front of an audience to speak and looking down to discover you have on your under-wear—and that's ALL!

The audience is a mirror of the speaker. Where do you see speakers address large groups most often? Do you ever notice the speaker that seems most at ease is the favored speaker for that audience? And the speaker who seems most up tight causes the audience to rejoice when that speaker sits down! Happy speakers tend to produce happy audiences and passionate speakers tend to produce passionate audiences. You can always predict the type of response during the Invitation Hymn at a southern revival by the type of delivery of the preacher. If it was a mundane and routine delivery, the congregation will dutifully sing the closing song without much response. If it was a fetching soul-searching delivery by a preacher who spoke to your heart and looked into your eyes, you may just sing "Just As I Am" for twenty minutes! Listen as the departing people meet the speaker at the back door of the church with comments like, "You were talking right to me" and "Thanks, I needed that". Just words, you say. That's right! Just words delivered in a fashion that compels the listener to focus and respond!

When someone is addressing a group and looking directly at you, it seems as though the comments are for <u>YOU</u>! Each audience you encounter will be made up of YOU. Every person in the group is a YOU. Successful communicators realize this! Especially during the tender opening moments of a presentation, you-talk is very necessary. Each person in the audience is probably thinking this applies to someone else. As a communicator, it's your duty to convince them of their own need for it. When you choose examples and comparisons for your presentation, remember the <u>YOU</u> sitting there listening. Say it to <u>YOU</u>! Say it with words <u>YOU</u> can understand! And speak to <u>YOU</u>, not to 'them'. 'Them' represents the other guy! You know, the one we all watch out for on two-lane roads after midnight. When a speaker uses the 'them' word, he immediately excludes his audience from any duty to pay attention to the comments. Most of all, remind <u>YOU</u> of the reward for buying the ideas or following the procedures outlined in the presentation.

It's one thing to personalize your comments, and you should, but when you look at your audience the result is even stronger. Politicians are required to read their speeches for legal and other reasons. Many of them have mastered the art of reading from a teleprompter so it will appear that they are looking at the camera or at the audience. How do you feel when you're in a conversation with a person who won't look at you or who is constantly interrupting their comments to you so they may speak with someone else? Makes you feel like you're not very important, or that whatever they're telling you is pretty insignificant. Remember, the audience mirrors the speaker. If you read your presentation to your audience, they drift away from you even though your comments may be extremely important. The person on your leadership team at work with the most allegiance from the employees is likely the person who does the most looking at employees during conversation and during presentations. Looking at the person with whom you're communicating is just plain natural! Look at every person in the audience. Look at the people on the right and the people on the left. Don't lock your gaze onto the friendly faces in the group, but keep looking around. YOU is the one you want to reach, and sometimes YOU isn't a happy or friendly person. Don't worry if several in your audience have a deadpan look. It isn't their job to look happy or friendly, it's yours!

People enjoy listening to a person as that person pours his heart out. Listen discretely as two friends converse on a quiet afternoon and you'll hear with your own ears. They may talk quietly until one expresses excitedly their approval or disapproval of some issue. They may even pause after this startling interjection, then return to the conversation. They'll even get loud on some issues. But people who know each other talk that way! If some of the goals of effective communication would be to cause the listener to feel comfortable listening and compelled to grasp the information, shouldn't communicators sound more like people in a conversation and less like barkers on a midway? Speakers intensify their effectiveness when they vary the rate, pitch and volume of their delivery. Talk high, talk low, talk fast and talk slow. Don't read! Talk! If the natural way for something to be said is loudly, say it loudly! If the natural way for something to be said is quietly, draw the microphone close and whisper it! When you say something to a group that should incite some sort of response, pause momentarily for that response to take place.

Watch those same two friends as they describe some situation or object. They make all sorts of gestures with their faces and hands. They may silhouette some object to give each other an idea of the shape of whatever they're discussing. Nothing helps bring a point home better than the same efforts from a speaker. When you speak of dimensions, use your hands. When expressing an emotion, use your face.

Some speakers make no gestures at all. Imagine a conversation between you and a friend where he stands like some sort of statue and deliver the information to you in one tone as he reads it from a paper. "That's not a conversation!" you say. "A conversation is relaxed and animated and comes from the heart!" Most folk will kindly sit there and tolerate your presentation, but a change comes. People can tell when you're using choreographed gestures. They know when you're reading someone else's feelings from a page. When people feel they are watching a performance, they mentally detach from it. Likewise, when they feel they are being scolded, they quietly detach and their pupils constrict. Inside, their self-image says to them "What does HE know! What does SHE know! Sure they say that! That's what they're SUPPOSED to say! They don't care about me! They don't even know me!" So much for influencing people to adopt a new procedure, reach certain goals or to forsake their wicked ways.

Remember the conversation of the two friends. Throughout the conversation, the voice inflection and gestures were genuine and natural. The pauses were genuine and natural. When speakers relax and communicate, audiences relax and involve themselves in the communication. They can tell when you believe what you're saying and believe in those you're saying it to.

As you go through your day-to-day business life, you encounter the leaders. Some of them are asking, some are telling, but all are communicating. They ask you for information or for help, or even for money! They give you a list of tasks and tell you things you'll need to know in order to complete those tasks today. When you encounter difficulty, they communicate encouraging even threatening words. The leaders communicate more often than they do any other thing. If you're destined for management, your communicative skills are going to determine just how high you'll go and how well you'll do once you're there.

Leader, as you communicate with your followers remember who those people are! You're talking to YOU. That's who you used to be!

Keep your personal priorities in focus

Chapter nine

Life's Greatest Quest

Throughout this book, you and I have explored our most wonderful asset—people! Some people have become very dear to us in this life. Family, loved ones, even friends at work are a vital and enriching part of our world. Sooner or later, you will have to give one of these people up. Life is short. We never seem to realize that until life is over. All people mourn the loss of their loved ones at a time of death. Death may come suddenly and unexpectedly, or at the end of a long illness. In the city or in the country, it makes your heart hurt when you face the fact you will never again hear the voice or feel the touch of that special person you are saying goodbye to. What a void it creates when someone very dear to you passes away!

If you ever attend a funeral in rural eastern North Carolina, you will have an interesting experience. Down in North Carolina, we all gather at the church house for the funeral. Most of us try to get there at least half an hour early, otherwise you may have to stand. For about an hour prior to the service, the casket remains open. Gone is the mindless clutter and hip-hop racket that has crept into so many Worship centers in our land. The organist or pianist will softly play the great old hymns with the deep meaning. As you sit and listen, your mind goes back to the days when you were growing up. Whether you're 30 or 90, you sit there and mentally sing them all again.

As folks arrive for the service, they file by the open casket for a final glimpse of this one who was such an important part of their lives. Whether a distant cousin, co-worker, Sunday School Class member, old flame from school or a neighbor, everybody sits quietly and remembers some special blessing that person brought to their life. Sometimes, the folks attending will quietly whisper among themselves about the last words of the departed loved one. Seems like the last words always have something to do with God or with their family. Matter of fact, I can't remember a single time when someone has told me the last words of a person were, "We sure did great on that fourth quarter, didn't we!" or "Tell me again, what is my net worth?"

Just as the hour for the funeral is reached, the preacher will ask the congregation to stand and sing as the family files in and takes their seats. We may sing "When We All Get To Heaven" or "Victory In Jesus" or some other great hymn of the faith. Even though you may have sung these songs over and over, the words suddenly take on a new meaning. You realize your friend is with Jesus. Now.

Then during the funeral, along with wonderful memories during the loved one's eulogy, the preacher always reminds us of how short life is compared to eternity. Without exception, he speaks of the faith of the loved one whose loss we mourn. Sometimes, the preacher will tell some personal story of a moment in the life of this person when their faith in God was deepened because it sustained our departed friend during his walk through some dark valley. As I sit there and drink in this moment, I'm always reminded of the truly important things in life.

At the close of the short service, the preacher will once again ask the congregation to stand and sing as the family leaves for the cemetery. The song is usually another great hymn like "Amazing

Grace" or "Blessed Assurance". By the time you leave the building, you *know* you've been to church. I may miss a wedding, I may even miss a Sunday or two during the year, but I NEVER miss a funeral. It reminds me to live life to the max, and to put all my emphasis in the right areas. Because, sooner than I may wish, they'll be singing for my family to come into the church house.

God becomes very important to you at a funeral, especially when the funeral is for someone you will miss terribly. That's understandable because you are an American and God is the most important part of the American Dream.

Some wonder how it was that the founding fathers, with all the extreme conditions they endured and the many loved ones whose funerals they attended, could have had so much character and fortitude. Solomon, in one of his stronger moments, put it down on paper in Proverbs 29:18, "Where there is no vision, the people perish." Meaning, where there IS vision the people survive and thrive! Our ancestors survived based upon the hope that was in their hearts rather than the stuff that was in their yards and homes. What was the overwhelming source of that hope during America's early days? It was their ever present faith in Almighty God.

Look at the words of our founding fathers, like George Washington and Benjamin Franklin. Read the records of the Supreme Court of the United States of America.

Unfortunately, most of this information is missing from the textbooks of American students. Secular humanists have systematically removed it over a period of less than 50 years. When I make mention of the Supreme Court, you may even cringe (thinking that NOTHING promoting God could EVER come from the liberal Supreme Court—inventors of the Separation of Church and State Doctrine). But American Statesmen and the Supreme Court were not always comprised of those who preferred to lift up feeble man and put down omnipotent God. At one point in our history as a nation, they wanted very much to pass faith in God on to you and to me.

91

In the minds and hearts of our early Supreme Court, every right and every law came from God. They believed America was a Christian nation! Their decision in the case <u>The Church Of The Holy Trinity vs. The United States</u>, reads in part, "Our laws and our institutions must necessarily be based upon, and embody the teachings of the Redeemer of Mankind. It is impossible that it be otherwise. And in this sense and of this extent our civilization and institutions are emphatically Christian." Quoting 87 precedents, they noted there were over 150 available. The early members of the Supreme Court protected and defended the hope they had inherited.

You probably have a tough time accepting this since the Supreme Court invented the doctrine of Separation of Church and State in 1947, citing NO precedents! What a difference a century and a half makes in the mindset of public servants. And what a difference in the mindset of our youth who have been educated in the absence of God.

Speaking of man's wisdom replacing God's, in 1884 a school wishing to teach morality in the absence of the Bible brought their case before the Supreme Court. In the case, the high court asked, "Why may not the Bible and especially the New Testament be read and taught as divine revelation in the school? Where can the purest principals of morality be learned so clearly or so perfectly as from the New Testament?" The Court ruled, in essence, that the absence of Christianity made it impossible to teach morals. That's a far cry from the definition of the word "is".

George Washington, our first president and the president of the convention that brought us our Constitution, said in his inaugural address, "The smiles of heaven can never be expected on any nation that disregards the eternal rules of order and right which heaven itself has ordained." In his farewell address, possibly one of the greatest speeches ever made by an American president, he said, "Of all the habits and dispositions which lead to political prosperity, religion and morality are indispensable supports. In vain would that man claim the tribute of patriotism who should labor to subvert these great pillars." George Washington wanted all Americans to live in the hope of prosperity and peace that can only thrive in a Godly nation.

John Quincy Adams said, "The highest glory of the American Revolution was that it connected in one indissoluble bond the principals of civic government with the principals of Christianity." John Quincy Adams wanted Americans to know a government operating on Christian principals was a government that had hope for success.

Maintaining a relationship with God wasn't merely a vogue social statement in the early days of our nation, it was considered essential to one's successful personal existence! Over 90 percent of the quotes of statesmen during the first 50 years of our nation's existence were Biblical quotes.

During the Constitutional Convention, our ancestors were working diligently to draw up our Constitution. After a long period of time the meeting reached an impasse. Realizing the importance of that instrument of freedom, Benjamin Franklin called the session into prayer, citing Psalm 127:1, "Except the Lord build the house, they labor in vain who build it." Our founding fathers physically got on their knees and asked Almighty God to intervene that we might have a Constitution. And He did. And we do.

Following the terrorist attack on America in September of 2001, President George W Bush cited the remainder of that same verse, "Unless the Lord watches over the city, they that guard it guard in vain", as reason for Americans to turn to God as our never ending source of hope. He repeatedly told us publicly that he was praying for America. And he encouraged all Americans to pray to Almighty God for our land.

According to the highest authority, someday, "In a moment, in the twinkling of an eye", the heavens will open and the Lord will return to this earth. The dead in Christ will rise, then the living in Christ will join them. At that time, all the earthly things we have worried about will suddenly fall into perspective. Their unimportance will be so obvious we'll view them, if we think of them at all, like we remember the last time we mowed the lawn. The priorities placed on all those tasks, the meetings we juggled, the clubs we were active in, the people we impressed, the automobiles and boats we got ourselves into debt for over and over, the house we changed or replaced so many times, the money we saved and invested - all those things that seemed so important and unavoidable will fade into insignificant events in an unimportant life. On that day, what we did with Jesus Christ will be the most important decision and series of events in our lives.

Whatever you believe, GOD made you and you will someday see him. He's going to ask you what you did with your life. He's going to say, "Depart from me" or "Well done." His decision will hinge *not* on what you did with your business, your family or even with your brain. His decision *will* hinge on what you did in your heart with Jesus Christ.

You can't be good enough to work your way into heaven! Jesus paid that price for you with his death on the Cross of Calvary. Because the very son of GOD loved you enough to die for you, you can't possibly be *bad* enough to go to Hell *if you accept His grace by giving your heart to Him.* Stop trying to justify your heavenly destination by being good. You can't! It won't work! Stop beating your heart up for all the mistakes you've made and are still making. They don't matter! Stop trying to fit into someone's mold of expectation for your acceptance as a Christian, their opinion doesn't count!

Jesus, the Son of GOD, died for YOU. He did that because He wanted you to have a choice to love and accept Him. When you accept His salvation, you choose to spend the never-ending span of Eternity with Him. You will never be sad, sick, depressed, overextended, rejected or even tired. And, you will never die. Once you make that choice to let him have your heart, the burdens of this life become much lighter and less important. The mission of this life becomes *ACCOMPLISHING WHAT GOD WANTS ME TO ACCOMPLISH WITH THE TALENTS AND RESOURCES HE HAS GIVEN ME.*

Plain, isn't it? When you start living each day for the LORD, things change. You still have daily priorities that become crises, people still disapprove of you and your ideas, you still make mistakes in your decisions, you still do things you shouldn't do. The difference is you *now* have an ever present consultant - Jesus Christ - upon whom you may call at any time. The line is never busy. His system is never down. He never gets tired of you and all of your problems. Jesus is always just a prayer away. HE doesn't stand on formality, either. HE hears your thoughts as you work at your keyboard, drive your car, walk or jog, embrace the person you love most in this world, walk into the boss's office to be fired, leave the doctor's office with a bad report, mow your lawn or play with your children. There is no moment in your life when he is not there, *wishing* you would reach out to him.

Oh, I know, you've been saving all your reaching out for Sunday morning at 11 AM. HE's there too! But church is just a filling station where you, along with the other believers, go to be refreshed in your faith. Church is supposed to be about God but God is not limited to church.

If you knew you could go to your local bank and withdraw as much money as you want with your ATM card (not have it charged against your account but have it freely, legally, openly to do with as you wish) would you only take out $100 a week or $200? No way! Sooner or later, you'd get so used to having all the money you want, you'd be showing up with a big bag or a truck! When you realize the impact of a life centered around the will of your LORD, you'll start calling on him several times a day or several times an hour. What a wonderful alternative to sitting at your desk and wondering what in the world you're going to do about the latest crisis! What a wonderful resource for bringing encouragement and leadership to your employees.

Some folks confuse this lifestyle with a Holier-than-thou attitude. Ever meet someone like that? It's a wonder *anyone* chooses to give his or her life to the LORD with that type of expectation. The idea that I've decided to give up everything and assume a lifestyle of Spartan existence while I pick on everyone I know for each little thing in their life that I don't approve of is scary to me.

It also puts a lot of responsibility on me. Now, I have to save the world! But if the only life I can answer for is mine, if Jesus has assured me I am His and we will be together for Eternity and if Jesus has told me He'll forgive me of *anything* I confess to *HIM* and ask His forgiveness of, the pressure to be perfect is off.

Every great American I have ever met has had some sort of intimate relationship with the Lord. I don't mean they talked like a TV Evangelist! They knew who God was and relied on Him to give meaning to their lives. They thanked God for their blessings and asked God to help them through their daily decisions. They spoke with God in their heart many times through the day. The great Americans I've know have literally walked through each day with God.

Genesis 5:24 speaks of Enoch as a man who walked with God. One day, he just didn't come back. What a way to go! Walk with God until one day you just walk right on into heaven. Live your life as though every day will be your last. Do your work as though every task will be your last. Love your family as though every expression of love will be your last. That's how Enoch lived and it was the lifestyle of those great Americans who have handed down this wonderful heritage in which we prosper. They lived like God was always watching and was always just itching to help.

You are indeed fortunate. You live in the free enterprise system, surrounded by the liberty of The United States of America. How well you live is ultimately your choice! You are free to choose a meaningful life of doing your best and enjoying the rewards of your efforts. Best of all, you are free to reach out to a God who loves you without reservation. Now that's the American Dream!

Perhaps you're one of those people that will take a book from the shelf and read the last few pages (to see if you'll like the book). If so, don't buy this book. If you read this entire final chapter, you've already read the most valuable information included in it.

Rags to Riches!
That's the American Dream!

Starting out in the Stock Room and working your way to the Board Room can be a fast ride with little or no time for leadership training.

Are you leading with little or no training?

Need fresh ideas on how to effectively lead and motivate your employees?

You'll benefit from these
Simple and practical ideas for working leaders!

Tim Dannelly, Professional Speaker, has worked for the US Air Force as a Non-Commissioned Officer and as a Government Contractor. He has managed radio stations and automobile dealerships. His leadership and management exposure includes sales professionals, entertainers and specialized technicians.

About the Author

Tim Dannelly

Tim Dannelly travels the United States speaking to salespeople, US and State Government agencies, and various civic and church organizations. He has well over thirty years experience in the areas of sales, public relations and broadcasting.

A native of Texas, Tim grew up in coastal North Carolina. He served his country in Vietnam, Virginia and Texas. While a member of the Air Force, he originated a nationally aired Air Force Recruiting radio program, which he also hosted.

He has owned his own small business, with over 80 employees, and has successfully turned around failing businesses for several owners. His management background includes corporate as well as private broadcast, real estate and automotive sales organizations.